The ❸ Therapies of
LIFE

Life-Changing Classics, VOLUME XXX

The ❸ Therapies
of
LIFE

Charlie
"Tremendous"
Jones

Foreword By: Tracey C. Jones

Life-Changing Classics, Volume XXX
The Three Therapies of Life

Published by
Tremendous Leadership
P. O. Box 267
Boiling Springs, PA 17007
717-701-8159 • 800-233-2665
www.TremendousLeadership.com

Copyright © 2018 Tremendous Leadership
All rights reserved.

ISBN: 978-1-949033-00-7

TABLE OF CONTENTS

Foreword by Tracey Jones 7

Biography of Charlie Jones 11

The Three Therapies 17

SUBHEADINGS

Talk to the Heart
and Not to the Ears 18

Learn to Laugh at Your Failures 22

Learn to be Thankful 23

Think Rather Than Just Listen 26

Introducing
The Three Therapies of Life 29

Therapy Number One: People 31

Therapy Number Two: Music	35
Therapy Number Three: Work	42
The Secret of Laughter	45
The Power of Books	51
What Books Taught Me About Patton's Life	55
What Books Taught Me About Lincoln's Life	56
What Books Taught Me About Chambers' Life	58
29 Other Life-Changing Classics	61

FOREWORD

Everyone should be in therapy. It's good for the body, mind, and soul. It helps unpack the baggage and enables us to deconstruct the mysteries that vex us in life. In *The Three Therapies of Life*, Charlie "Tremendous" Jones shares practical and applicable ways to heal yourself so you can continue to impact others and change lives. I uncovered this material from a DVD I found. It was recorded back in the '90s when my father was in his heyday (which was technically every day). In this message, he spoke to an audience of fellow speakers and presenters at the National Speakers Association (NSA). His words rang truer to my ears and

THE 3 THERAPIES *of* LIFE

heart than they ever had before. I guess I needed some "Tremendous" therapy.

This Life-Changing classic is pure "Tremendous;" real, down-to-earth, humorous, and spoken from the heart. In a world where it so often appears that everyone is having the best day of their life and has it all figured out, my father lets us know it's okay if you're not. He is a practitioner of the highest order. He has changed so many lives because he has lived so many lives. His compassion for sharing others' heartaches while exhorting and giving them the means to overcome them are the ties that bind all of us together. His signature "tell it like it is" style, coupled with some timeless truths, make this little gem one that you'll turn to for years to come.

Let these three therapies minister to your life. They're free, they're universal, and they're guaranteed. These therapies will speak to you in your walk and help you process your own unique situation. Life is a flowing river that's constantly changing. The broken heart is the one that is open to therapy. When I think of my father, I do not envision the consummate success or famous speaker. What I do see and hear is a humble man who mastered the joy of longsuffering and used his gifting to exhort others to do the same. I hope that you see and hear it as well, and that it blesses you.

Tracey Jones
President
Tremendous Leadership

BIOGRAPHY OF CHARLIE "TREMENDOUS" JONES

Charlie "Tremendous" Jones entered the gates of Heaven on October 16, 2008. He made his mark as a best-selling author, publisher, and internationally acclaimed motivational speaker who gained a reputation as an inspirational humorist and book evangelist.

Charles E. Jones was born in Alabama and grew up in Pennsylvania. His beloved wife Gloria resides in Mechanicsburg, Pennsylvania. Their marriage produced six children and seven grandchildren.

THE **3** THERAPIES *of* LIFE

Before achieving tremendous success as a motivational speaker, Charlie Jones started off as an insurance salesman. In 1950—just one year after entering the insurance business with one of America's top-ten companies—he was awarded his agency's Most Valuable Associate award at the age of 23. Ten years later Mr. Jones received his company's highest management award for recruiting, manpower and development, and business management.

At age 37 his organization exceeded $100 million in force, at which time he founded Life Management Services to share his experiences through seminars and consulting.

For more than a quarter of a century, thousands of audiences in America, Canada, Mexico, Australia, New Zealand, Europe, and Asia experienced nonstop laughter as Mr. Tremendous shared his ideas about life's most challenging situations in business and at home.

He is the author of *Life Is Tremendous,* a best-selling book about his 7 Laws of Leadership, with more than 3 million copies in print. Two of his speeches—"The Price of Leadership" and "Where Does Leadership Begin?"—have been enjoyed by millions on audio recordings and at conventions.

He was featured on a variety of radio programs, television networks, and films ranging from the *Dynamic Achievers World Network* television series to the *Insights into Excellence* video training series.

The University of Southern California, University of Tennessee, and Pensacola Christian College are just a few of the institutions where Mr. Jones was featured as a guest lecturer.

He also served on the advisory boards of several organizations and was the president and founder of Life Management Services Inc.

In addition to being a dynamic speaker and businessman, Mr. Jones was also a great humanitarian, with a passion for helping individuals understand the value of reading. It was Mac McMillon whom Mr. Jones first heard say, "You are the same today as you'll be five years from now except for two things: the people you meet and the books you read." This statement eventually became one of Mr. Jones's most quoted lines as he inspired individuals all over the world to read.

Through his publishing company and bookstore, Executive Books, Mr. Jones gave away millions of books, fulfilling his mission as a book evangelist. In addition to the generous donations the company still makes, the business that Mr. Tremendous originated is presently thriving under the direction of his daughter, Tracey Jones.

For more than 50 years Charlie "Tremendous" Jones was passionate about exciting people to read, think, and share. In 2002 he received a Doctor of Humane Letters degree from Central Pennsylvania College, and in 2003 the college's new library was named the

Biography of Charlie "Tremendous" Jones

Charles "T" Jones Leadership Library in recognition of his love for reading and sharing great books.

In 2013, the Charles and Gloria Jones Library was unveiled in the Teague Learning Commons at Lancaster Bible College located in Lancaster, PA. This library also hosts the Oswald Chambers reading room in honor of Mr. Jones' deep appreciation of this author.

THE THREE THERAPIES OF LIFE

Before I delve into the three therapies of life, I would like to talk about how to achieve excellence through thinking with people. Have you ever been speaking to a group or sharing with a prospect and you are so excited you're about to leap out of your shoes? Then you notice someone sleeping during your presentation?

Don't feel bad. They used to sleep when I talked too, but never on the front row! I noticed this and would ask myself, "Why are they sleeping? Why are they not listening?" It took years, but I finally figured it out for me. Now, you just have to figure it out for you. They were not listening to me because I had a bad habit of talking to people's ears. Everybody knows you hear with your ears, but you see with your eyes and you learn with your heart. Since I had only been talking to their ears, their eyes decided they had nothing to do but close for a while.

Talk to the Heart Not to the Ears

It's all right to talk about how to speak to the ear, but you better make sure you go to the heart. You know why some teachers don't teach? They talk to children's ears and not to their hearts. Do you know why some pastors never reach their flock? They talk to people's ears and not to their hearts. You know why some managers and salespeople never reach the prospect or the trainee? They focus on the ear, not on the heart. You'll find if you're going to enjoy this word *excellence* in your life, you'd better be learning a technique. One of the greatest lessons you'll learn in dealing with people is to go to the ear with the point, and then go to the heart with an illustration. This will help them see with their heart what they heard with their ear. Then you watch their eyes to light up and they say, "I see what you mean." When they really see what you mean, their lips curl up, and they smile.

Now, to make this point, let me tell you a little story. Have you ever heard the expression, "You brought it on yourself?" Are you married? Then you might hear it often. My wife is always telling me, "You brought it on yourself. You brought it on yourself." I say, "I know I brought it on myself. I don't need your flack." You know why my wife is so brutal to me? Because she's not on commission! If my wife were on commission she would treat me like I treat my prospects!

Now, suppose you're my prospect or you're one of my staff. We have a problem. You brought it on yourself. You know you brought it on yourself, I know you brought it on yourself, and you know I know you brought it on yourself. Do you think I'm going to tell you, "You brought

THE 3 THERAPIES *of* LIFE

it on yourself?" No. Why? I know how it sounds and I don't like it either.

Now, once in a while you hear somebody say, "I tell them to their face like it is." I say, "Well, then you go to work for our competition. We don't need you around here." If you're going to tell people something to their face and it involves their feelings, you better go to their heart and help them see. I love to *see* where I'm wrong. You love to *see* where you're wrong. But isn't it horrible to have to *hear* you're wrong?

Now, here's my technique. If I told you that you brought it on yourself, there would be confrontation, argument, and divisiveness. You'll respond with, "I don't have time for this!" Now, I'm going to tell a story in a way that when any man hears it, he's going to see how he brought it on himself. If I told him he brought it on himself, he wants to fight. But if I tell a story, he'll hear it, and he'll see that *he* brought it on himself, and he'll be falling off his chair laughing. You'll find if you're going to have excellence in what you do, the key will be laughter and encouraging others to take positive action, rather than arguing about why they're not justified in receiving this kind of criticism.

There's a story about two carpenters who sit down every day to eat their lunch. One guy starts eating his sandwiches. The other guy opens up his sandwiches and every day he has peanut butter sandwiches. He hates peanut butter sandwiches! Every day when he sees the peanut butter sandwiches he shouts, "Oh, no! Not this again! Peanut butter sandwiches! I hate peanut butter sandwiches! I can't take it anymore!" Well, one day his buddy had enough. He says, "Joe, if you hate peanut butter sandwiches so much, why don't you tell your wife you don't like peanut butter sandwiches?" To which Joe replied, "You leave my wife out of this. I pack my own lunch!"

Have a good laugh, friend.

Learn to Laugh at Your Failures

If you're going to have a great life while you do a great job, you need to learn how to laugh at your failures. Laughing at your failures doesn't mean you like to fail. It means if you're not learning how to laugh and build on your heartaches, you'll never do much.

Once a young man asked me, "Mr. Jones, what's an ingredient of success?"

"Good judgment," I replied.

"How do you get that?"

"Experience."

"How do you get that?"

"Poor judgment."

You cannot like to fail, but if you're not learning how to laugh and build on your heartaches, you're not even in the game. Also, if you're going to have a great life while you do a great job, you need to learn how to get people to laugh at themselves.

I get a lot of criticism, and this goes with what I do as a speaker and motivator. Some people say, "You know the trouble with you, Charlie Jones, is that you're always kidding." That's right. But anybody who is around me knows I'm always serious too. You see, if you're going to be serious, you'd better learn how to make things lighter because they're carrying a heavy enough load already without you burdening them more. Also, life is not a joke. So you just can't go around just having fun without being serious.

Here are some basic things you need to learn and apply all through your life's journey if you're going to be effective.

Learn to Be Thankful

The first mark of greatness is *thankfulness*. So, first and foremost, be grateful. The first sign of smallness is *thanklessness*. But an attitude of gratitude flavors everything you do.

Once in a while, some young tiger will say to me, "Did you used to feel this

THE 3 THERAPIES *of* LIFE

way years ago when you didn't have anything?" I used to go home and I'd say, "Look, honey. Look! Look! Man of the Month. Look at this, Man of the Year!" She'd say, "Where's the cash?" I'd say, "Honey, you listen here. If we don't start learning to be happy when we've got nothing, we will never be thankful and happy when we have everything." I'm glad I can tell you this today, simply as a thinker and a fellow learner, and not as someone trying to sell you something. I hope because we are thinking and laughing together, you are more grateful and thankful.

Sometimes when we're with the children and giving thanks we say something like this: "Dear God, we thank you for our food. We want you to know if we had no food we would thank you just the same because, God, we want you to know we're not thankful for just what you give us. We're thankful, most of all, for the privilege of just learning to be thankful." More is said from a thankful heart than will ever be said with any mind—no matter how brilliant you are.

In addition to being thankful, be committed. Don't ever speak just because you like to speak. It's all right to speak because you like to speak, but the main reason you should speak is because you *have to* speak. If you pay me, pay me, but if you don't pay me, I'm speaking anyway.

It is also important to memorize. Know your talks upside, downside, inside, outside, and then personalize it. Make sure a little of your heartache comes through so they can identify with you because you personalized it. If you are going to be doing this all your life, realize what you're saying. People say to me, "How can you give the same talk?" I've given one talk 2,500 times. Then they ask, "How can you do that and make it fresh every time?" It's because I never gave that talk to an audience. *The Price of Leadership* message --that's *my* heart. That's *my* life. I give that *for me*.

THE 3 THERAPIES *of* LIFE

It wouldn't matter if anybody agreed or liked a word of it. That's for me.

Think Rather Than Just Listen

Now that I gave you my points, let's get down to work. How would you like a guarantee that you'll never hear another weak lecture, dry sermon, or poor speaker as long as you live? Wouldn't you like that?

When giving a live talk I say, "Everybody, get out your pens, you'll need it. Okay, are you ready? Got your pens?" Ready, here it is! "Don't you write down one word I say!" You say, "You're not going to say anything worth writing down in almost an hour?"

Do you know why I don't want you to write down anything I say? It's because I'm going to prove to you, that for the most part, what you hear does not do you any good.

Do you know how I can prove this? Easy! Because you know if what you hear did you any good, you'd be a whole lot better than what you are. After all, you've sure heard enough, haven't you?

All my life I've been dragged out to meetings and seminars and all I've ever heard is, "Listen! Listen! Listen!" And I listen! And listen! And listen! And the more I listened, the more confused I got! And one day I caught on. I wasn't supposed to just listen—ha!

You say, "Well what were you supposed to do?" You are supposed to *think*. Good speakers can be a menace, and some are. The number one objective with an audience is not getting them to just listen, but to think. Have you ever heard of this one? "Do you know that people only remember 10 percent of what you said 10 minutes after you said it?" You know what I say to that? That's too much!

Do you know the greatest compliment you can pay me? It's when you leave one of my speeches and say, "Charlie Jones, I don't remember one word you said, but I don't remember an hour when I had more fun laughing at my heartaches and

THE **3** THERAPIES *of* LIFE

seeing things more clearly that I always knew, but didn't know I knew." That's the greatest thing you'll ever do for anybody.

From now on, when a speaker begins to speak, when a lecturer begins to lecture, when a pastor begins to preach, take out your pen, make a few notes of what you thought you heard. But save most of the room to make notes of what you *thought* as a result of what you heard. In other words, just leave your mind in neutral for a little bit as you listen and then let it be stimulated and activated to get those thoughts rolling. Help put some new words on those old thoughts that are laying there dormant so they can get to your mind to think them through. Then think them out loud with your lips and see how little you know about what you're saying so you can rethink and unlearn it and keep growing.

In church, I do this. When our pastor begins to speak, I begin making notes of things I think. This excites our pastor. He thinks I'm writing down his sermon! Sometimes I think he should throw away his sermon and get my notes. And then, going out of church, I shake him up and say, "Pastor, you were really good this morning. You interrupted my train of thought half a dozen times!"

What is managing? Managing is interrupting a person's train of thought. What is selling? Selling is interrupting a prospect's train of thought. What's preaching? What's teaching? Teaching is interrupting the train of thought to get students to discover what they knew. We do not pump it in; we become a catalyst, an activator to bring it out. What a difference.

Introducing The Three Therapies of Life

Okay. So now we're ready to think. What can we share that would fit all different types of people: the veterans, the rookies, the successes, and the ones who are starting? I thought I'd share with you the greatest thing I've been learning in the many years I've been working with people.

THE 3 THERAPIES *of* LIFE

I started selling *Liberty* magazines when I was six years old to work my way through kindergarten. Based on my decades of experience, I will spend a few moments on something that's been good for me over the years: the three therapies of life—*people*, *music*, and *work*. Now the beautiful part about these three therapies is, you can't buy them. You can't earn them. You can't learn them. God builds them all in and you get a choice. You can learn to *act them out* and to *show how good* you're doing, or you can *commit your life* to *live them out*.

Don't worry when you hear talk about hard times. You know why? If you're learning the three therapies of life and using them every day, you'll know that your worst years were always your best years. And if you're not learning these three therapies, you'll discover your best years will always be your worst years. But if you're learning the three therapies, it won't matter whether it's a good or bad year. It'll always be a good year for you.

Therapy Number One: People

What is the first therapy of building a great life? The first therapy is *people*. There is a song that says, "People, people who need people, are the luckiest people in the world." You say, "Well you don't *know* the kind of people I'm working with." Well they didn't *know* when they got you either. It looks about even to me.

People used to come into my office and we'd have the following conversation:

"Mr. Jones, I'm going to quit."

"Well, why do you want to quit this time?" I reply.

"I don't like the people I'm working with."

"Well that doesn't surprise me. They just told me yesterday how they hated you. Now listen. You can't quit here because you hate people. You'll hate them anywhere. Stay here and hate them, go to work, and be quiet!"

THE **3** THERAPIES *of* LIFE

Can you believe that? I tell people, I hope you like people and I hope people like you, but we don't work with people because we like people. You know why we work with people? I'll tell you why. Because there's nothing else to work with, so go to work and shut up!

People. You need people when you're up. You need people when you're down. You know why so many speakers are happier than anybody else? Because their lives revolve around people—lots of people. Their lives are not any easier—how tough and miserable it is for some of them. But when your life is wrapped up in people, there is no therapy in the world like it. When you withdraw from people, you dig your own dungeon deeper and sign your death warrant.

Why do people have so much fun at conferences? Because you're in an atmosphere of people who dream and have hopes and ups and downs and you're feeling at home. Wonderful! But I have to get you ready for when you go home.

You might remember the problems you had when you left the office the other day, but wait 'til you get home!

What's the first red flag for Monday morning when you wake up? Red flag number one. Watch out for this one when you wake up and think, "Oh, I sure hope I don't have to talk to many people today." Red flag number two. "I never get going 'til 10 in the morning." Well, stay in bed 'til 11! Work nights! "I never get going 'til the second cup of coffee." Well, start with the second! We're going bankrupt and you want a cup of coffee!

How about this one? A company advertises: Come to our event. We're having a great meeting! Some say, "I don't want to go." Why not? "I heard all that crap before." May I remind you, I don't care who the speakers are. If you had every great speaker in the world come, the reason you should go to a meeting is never to hear a speaker. They throw them in to fill up time and to charge you admission. I'll tell you the reason you should go.

THE 3 THERAPIES *of* LIFE

You go to be with other people like yourself—people of ups and downs, successes, failures, tears, and joys. You don't get it out of an audio recording or a book. You don't get it out of speakers. You get it by being with people. Look at how many of us over the years have greater relationships at a few meetings a year than you have in your own family? Don't ask me why that is. Everybody knows it is.

How about this one—when someone says: "You know the people that ought to be here today are the people that aren't here." Wrong. The people that ought to be there are the people that are there. The people that aren't there—thank God they didn't come. Right! And maybe a couple of you should have stayed home.

I guess I'm the luckiest person ever born. You know why? When you were born in the '20s and raised in the early '30s, you know what you learned? You learned you didn't have anything but people. Oh God, I'm so thankful. In the old days I used to be so jealous of everyone else because we had nothing. As the years went by, I realized I had something better than nothing. I had everything. If you didn't have fun with people, you'd sing. If you didn't learn how to play and invent your own things, you didn't have anything. People. God thank you for people and for when we learn that we can't walk away from people. Oh how many times I wanted to give up on people. How wonderful it is when you're locked in and you need them not because you like them and not because they love you. You need them because they're people just like you.

Therapy Number Two: Music

Therapy number two is *Music. Music. Music.*

May I share an idea on music? It'll save some of your lives, maybe even some of your marriages. Some of you know this better than I do. For others, it will be your first time to think a great truth, one you've always known. There'll come a time in your life someday, the crises, the humiliation, the tragedy will be

THE **3** THERAPIES *of* LIFE

so severe, there will be few things that can reach your need like music.

In life, there's a pendulum always swinging. It's swinging now. You can't see it, but it's swinging. It swings in the stock market. The pendulum swings in politics. Who'd believe what's happening in the world today? When the pendulum swings, it swings in spite of everything. It's the seasons of life.

The pendulum swings in government.

The pendulum swings in sports.

The pendulum swings in life.

I remember years ago when a colleague named Mr. Henry started speaking and they told him all the things to do. He listened to the audios. He read the books. He went to all the seminars. He went to the workshops. And what happened? Nothing! Then he just started to commit his life and did nothing—and what happened? Oh, the success came. I joke about how he now makes up all those lies about how he did it.

Now let's get personal. Let's get real personal. In your life, the pendulum swings. Several of you have told me that this has been the best year of your life. I believe for some of you it was the best year of your life. I say this because I want you to know that sometimes I'm as cynical as you are. But it was a good year. Some of you had the best year of your life and some of you are on cloud nine now because you've just gone through one of the best months of your life. You couldn't wait to share how the pendulum had swung. The tide has turned. I'm really happy for you. I'm happy with all my heart.

On the other hand, there are some people who've just had the worst year of their life. There are some right now going through the worst month of their life. Now remember, there's a lot of ways to have a bad month. It need not be in meetings or bookings. It need not be in income. It can be with your children, your marriage. It can be with your grandchildren or your health. There are lots of ways to have a bad month. If today you're hurting, I

THE **3** THERAPIES *of* LIFE

want to speak mainly to you. Excuse me, I want to *think* mainly with you. I want to remind you the pendulum swings. If you think your heart is so broken that there's no hope, you're wrong. Don't panic. The pendulum will swing back.

Now you know why I've always been able to deal more with failure than success with people? I have because that's the story of my life. All my life, it's been one heartache, one thing after another. I just can't believe anyone can make the mistakes I've made and still look a little successful. The only reason I've survived is not just because of things I did right, but all the things—by the grace of God—I discovered were wrong in the nick of time and then didn't do anything about it. So, I'm an authority in discouragement. I've gone on stage at Carnegie Hall or Caesar's Palace to speak to a convention when my heart ached so badly with discouragement, I could hardly breathe, and no one knew it. My wife never knew it. She suspected it, maybe, but she didn't know it.

Some of you are wondering, "Didn't you love your wife enough to tell her?" I loved her enough *not* to tell her. There are some things, my dear friend, you don't get out of by talking to anybody. You've got to love through it and sometimes, it never goes away. Other people have to know this and you need to help them know it.

A few times, I've reached such a low over months of discouragement, I felt like I couldn't even pray. You say, "Well I was never that low." You never had my problems, either—and you never had my mother-in-law. My mother-in-law is a test pilot at a broom factory. No she's not. Can't you tell when I'm kidding? That is a lie. My mother-in-law is not a test pilot at a broom factory, but it is true that at times in my life, when I've gone through some periods of financial or physical or marital challenges, I didn't know how to go on.

Here's a point I want to make. There will come times in your life where you

THE **3** THERAPIES *of* LIFE

might feel like you can't go on. You know what happens when you feel like you can't go on but you still won't give up? Do you know what you need? In addition to needing God, you need the thing God made that can bypass the ear and go straight to the heart. Music.

I just did a meeting about three or four months ago for a company that spent $1,800,000 on the meeting. They had a bad year, the worst in 50 years, and I had the closing hour. They told me for weeks in letters and personal interviews what they wanted. I went there a day ahead of time, and I saw what they told me they wanted but what I prepared was not what they needed. Believe me when I say, the strain was unbelievable. You know what you ought to do, and you know you can't do it, and you're drained. So, there I was at midnight in the office and I am drained. What did I do to get myself ready?

I put on some uplifting music. For one hour, I listened, woo! I'll tell you, after an hour of this *therapy*, I realized I knew what I needed to do, and whether or not they paid me didn't matter. I went to the meeting and I did the thing that needed to be done and it was fantastic. Why? Because I had to get *me* up. We created an atmosphere to help them enjoy all the great things that already had been done.

When I'm extremely tired, you know what I play? Bagpipes, bagpipes, oh Lord, I love bagpipes. There'll be bagpipes in heaven. You know how I know there'll be bagpipes in heaven? Because my mother-in-law hates bagpipes! I'm only kidding.

You know what some of you need to learn to do when you can't sleep? During those times when the more you try to sleep, the more you're awake, here's what you can do. I'll lie down and run old hymns through my mind, the old hymns of God's love and His kindness and patience. Music, music. I am very grateful for the devotions and the music they do at our conferences. I carry music in my briefcase. You must have music.

THE 3 THERAPIES *of* LIFE

Therapy Number Three: Work

Therapy number three is *work*! You say, "They're not paying me what I'm worth now." You better thank God for that; you would get nothing. You work if you get paid. You work if you don't get paid. You say, "I have a friend who doesn't have a job, what should he do?" Work! "You can't work without a job," you say. Don't tell me you can't work without a job. My dad, when I was a little boy, worked 18 hours a day. So what was his work? He had no work. He worked 18 hours a day looking for work. He worked at looking for work because he knew something that everybody has to learn some time in life. You don't work because you get paid. You work because it's your life. You need to work. If they pay you, get your pay. If they don't pay you, find some way to work. Why? Because you *can* work, work!

I get people telling me over and over again. "Well I'm 55 years old. I've only got 10 more good years left." You thumbsucker, go to work and shut up. 55? You're barely dry behind the ears! And then you hear a few out there today. There're not too many, but you'll hear a few say, "Well I'm 65 now. My life's almost over." Can you believe that?

Men like Cavett Robert, Dr. Norman Vincent Peale, and Ken McFarland had tremendous accomplishments in their latter years. I have had at least 26 tours of Australia. Every tour we've ever done over the years, there's been somebody on that tour over 65, 75, and 85. I hear this a lot, "I'm getting old." You're not getting old. You need to learn about work. When you learn about work, you'll discover life is good at 20. Life is better at 40. Life is better at 60. Life is better at 80.

You know what the trouble is with some of you young people? You work for money. You say, "What's wrong with that?" Nothing. You're allowed to work for money. The kids need tuition. You need a home. You need nice clothes and cars. You know when you begin to live? When you begin to work because it's your life. I gave

THE **3** THERAPIES *of* LIFE

1,500 talks before I ever got a nickel. For years, I did 25 talks in one week, a breakfast, lunch, and a dinner meeting and three on Sunday. In California, I donated a week every year for 10 years. I never got a penny. You said, "That's honorable." No, it's not honorable. I owed it. Had I not done that, I wouldn't have learned some things I couldn't learn except to give it away. It's just work.

You say, "Well how much money does a man need?" I say, just enough to keep your wife off your back. So, go to work. Ladies, don't you laugh. You have no right. Every time your poor husband comes home, "Honey! There you are. Honey, get me a condominium down in St. Petersburg." Men, take your wives down to St. Petersburg. Let them watch those old thumb-suckers sitting on the white benches with the dark glasses. They're all dead. They have no place to bury them all! I'll tell you where to take your wife. Take your wife up to Rockland, Maine; Duluth, Minnesota; Boise,

Idaho—where you have to keep moving to stay alive.

As I said, there are a lot of people in the world working for money and there is nothing wrong with this. But in terms of working to serve humanity, Mother Teresa is one of the finest examples of great devotion and dedication. How can she be so devoted to things like picking the lepers off the street? You say, "Doesn't she have something better to do than helping people that are already almost dead?" She has learned to do what you can, where you are, and forget all the other critics and people who have good advice. Just go do something. Work.

The Secret of Laughter

The greatest thing I've been learning all my life is that young people hurt, just like old people. I've been learning that rich people hurt just like poor people, and sometimes well people hurt like sick people. One of my greatest discoveries in life is that you can't take hurt out of life, even your own. But there are some ways

THE **3** THERAPIES *of* LIFE

to make hurt *better* rather than *bitter*, and most of you know that and some of you know it *better*. The greatest tool that God ever made to make hurt *better* rather than *bitter* is a tool called laughter.

So, remember, it isn't just having somebody to make you laugh. I love comedians, but I wouldn't want to be one, because they get paid getting people to laugh at them. But a good speaker is somebody who in addition to having a message—number one—he gets people to laugh a little at themselves. But not always telling jokes. Sometimes just a great truth makes you laugh. So the secret is laughter.

It's like when the guy said to his wife, "Honey, how can one woman be so beautiful and stupid?" She says, "God made me this way." He says, "Why would God make you so beautiful and stupid?" "Well he made me beautiful so you'd love me and stupid so I could love you."

You say, "Well, where do you get all these jokes, Charlie Jones?" My joke book. I'm not telling you to buy it, but I can tell you this: if everybody in America would buy this book—my joke book—it would mean a lot to me. It won't do much for you. It would mean a lot to my wife. I never cared about money. She wants it.

You say, "Well you know, that's one of my troubles. I'm a serious speaker. I can't tell jokes." That's why I wrote this book. You can read jokes to them now. Say, "Here, let me read you a joke." How about this one? "A man is incomplete until he's married. Then he's finished." How about this one. Do you have kids? This kid says, "Dad, Dad, everybody hates me." He says, "Son, don't say that. Everybody hasn't met you yet."

Okay, now wait. I'm going to prove something to you. You don't need to tell jokes. You don't need to be a comedian. Just read them a joke. I'm going to give you some more jokes now.

You say, "Where do you get all these jokes?" Everything I share with you, I'll show you the book where I got it from. Every young person, every old person, every rich

THE **3** THERAPIES *of* LIFE

person, every poor person, I want them to know no matter how poor you are, you can find great riches and a degree of excellence through the books you read if you'll realize them, not just memorize them.

You need humor. That joke about that stupid and beautiful wife—that's in my joke book. How about this one? She says, "Honey, the car is flooded." He says, "How do you know?" "It's in the swimming pool." It's in my joke book. He says, "How'd you get the car in the kitchen?" She says, "Easy. Turn left in the living room." It's in my joke book. If the joke bombs, it's in the book.

You see, friends, excellence is not determined by how strong you are in some area. It's using what you have to be a little bit better to get people to think with you. You'll get them thinking better if you get them laughing, but don't ever let them laugh at you. Comedians get paid to get people to laugh at them. Good managers, and teachers, and salespeople get people to laugh at themselves.

Well, let me give you one more then we'll call it a day. What every woman wants in a man is not necessarily what she's going to get. Every woman wants a man who's a brilliant conversationalist. She wants a sensitive man who is kind and understanding and truly loving. She wants a hardworking man who helps around the house while washing the dishes, vacuuming the floors, and taking care of the yard. She wants someone who helps her raise the children. She wants a man with emotional and physical strength. She wants a man who's as smart as Einstein but looks like Robert Redford. That's what you want, huh? Here's what some women will get.

He always takes her out to the best restaurants. Someday he may take her inside. He doesn't have ulcers. He gives them. Any time he gets an idea in his head he has the whole thing in a nutshell. He's well known as a miracle worker. It's a miracle when he works. He supports his wife in a manner in which she was accustomed. He's letting her keep her

THE **3** THERAPIES *of* LIFE

job. He's such a bore he even bores you to death when he gives you a compliment, and he has occasional flashes of silence that make his conversation brilliant.

Now, men, it's our turn. What every man wants in a woman is not necessarily what he's going to get. Every man wants a woman who's always beautiful and cheerful. Could've married a movie star, but wanted only you. She has hair that never needs curlers or beauty shops. She has beauty that won't ruin in a rainstorm. She's never sick. She's just allergic to jewelry and fur coats. She insists that moving the furniture by herself is good for her figure. She's an expert in cooking, cleaning the house, fixing the car, TV repair, painting the house, and keeping her mouth shut. Her favorite hobbies are mowing the lawn and shoveling snow. She hates credit cards. Her favorite expression is, "What can I do for you next, dear?" She thinks you have Einstein's brain but look like Mr. America. She wishes you would go fishing and golfing with the boys more often so she could get some sewing done. She loves you because you are so sexy.

That's what you want men, huh? Here's what some of you might get. She speaks 140 words a minute with gusts up to 180. She once was a model for a totem pole. She's a light eater. As soon as it gets light she starts eating. Where there's smoke, she's cooking. She lets you know you have only two faults, everything you say and everything you do. No matter what she does with it, her hair looks like an explosion in a steel wool factory. If you get lost, don't worry. Open your wallet. She'll find you in a hurry.

The Power of Books

Those of you who know me, know my trademark is books, because my objective in life is to get people to read and think. Therefore, I promote reading and hand out lots of books. This is because many years ago, I heard a man named Mac McMillan from Abilene, Texas. He had me laugh for an hour at my heartaches and identify with some principles that showed me that even though we had never met we were very much alike. Then he closed his talk and he said, "You are the same today as you'll be five years from now except for two things: the people you meet and the books you read."

The people you meet and the books you read. For decades I have said this every day, "You are the same today as you'll be five years from now except for the people you meet and the books you read."

Hang around achievers, you'll be a better achiever. Hang around thinkers, you'll be a better thinker. Hang around givers, you'll be a better giver. Hang around a bunch of thumb-sucking, complaining, griping boneheads, and you'll be a better thumb-sucking, complaining, griping, bonehead. Now, there's only one trouble with people; you can't take them home with you.

So that's why we talk about books. I can tell you this: every thought I share today, I can tell you the seed thought, which book, which biography it came from. I could tell you every one. You say, "Are you a fast reader?" I'm a slow reader. Sometimes it takes me a whole hour to read one page. You say, "I never knew anybody that slow." Well, you do now! You say, "Why are you so slow?" I don't know why I'm slow. I used to be ashamed of it, but I've got money now. I'm not ashamed.

Excellence. Oh, there are so many dimensions of excellence. There are so many great discoveries, but I'd have to say if I have to pick one, it would be the discovery of *thinking* because of the power of books. Everyone who knows me knows my trademark is books. As a salesman, it was books. As a manager, it was books. In my home, it's books. In my friends' lives, it's books. Years ago I had a habit—everybody would get a book. If you came across my path, you'd get a book.

The people you meet and the books you read...

At our meetings are some of the greatest, most influential people in all the

THE **3** THERAPIES *of* LIFE

world who have touched millions and millions of lives and I know that. But I know one thing. I don't care who your mentor or role model is in this group. You'll never learn about them by hanging around them. You never get to know somebody by just hanging around them. If I want to know what you're like, I'll find out who your role models were, who your heroes are, who your favorite authors were, and who shapes your life? That's what I'll do. I'll get to know you better than your mother knew you. I'll find out what you are inside out.

I love all the great leaders I have personally met over the years, but you know what? I can't take them home. I've got to go alone. But isn't it wonderful, aloneness? Aloneness.

Some people think they're lonely because they're young. Some people think they're lonely because they're old. Some people think they're lonely because they're poor. Some people think they're lonely because they're rich. Everybody gets lonely at times and that's the way it is because you discover out of loneliness a thing called aloneness. You grow alone. No woman grows for a man. No man grows for a woman. No parent grows for a child. When you grow, you grow alone.

What Books Taught Me About Patton's Life

Ah, to be alone with the books. Oh, I wish we could talk all day about books. How about General Patton—how I love him. General Patton said, "If you're all thinking alike somebody isn't thinking." When you're thinking, you're always discovering new dimensions of everything you ever said.

Mr. Patton said, "Don't be afraid to fear. Fear's like taking a cold shower. When the water is ice cold, don't tiptoe in. Leap in and spread the pain around." He also said, "The test of success is not what you do when you are on top. Success is how high you bounce when you hit the bottom."

THE 3 THERAPIES *of* LIFE

What Books Taught Me About Lincoln's Life

Abraham Lincoln. One of the most revered names today in the world. I think no name is so loved and respected as Abraham Lincoln. I guess you know Lincoln had no education. A lot of people tell you the secret of excellence is education. Well, I'm sure that has something to do with it. Lincoln had two years. You say, "If you're raised in a ghetto in a broken home, you don't have much of a chance." Lincoln was raised in worse than a ghetto. He didn't even have a door or a window on his cabin. The first year after his mother died they had a crawlspace. There were eight people to a room and they had no candlelight either.

Then there's a big thing on self-esteem today. Of course, I know the value of self-esteem, but Lincoln had none. How about self-image? Lincoln had no self-image. You say, "You need somebody to believe in you." Lincoln never had a soul. His mother died when he was a boy.

He never got to spend any time with his father. His sister died when she was in her teens. The first girl he loved died. The lady he married was a wonderful woman, but it was hell on earth because her parents hated him and felt that she should've married up and not down.

You say, "Well, the people loved him." The majority hated him. Only 40 percent of the popular vote chose Abraham Lincoln. He was elected by the electoral college. He was hated by the majority of the population. He was hated by most newspapers in America. Does that not cause you to wonder how a man with everything going against him could become one of the most revered names in the world?

He had a couple things going for him. Even though he never joined a church, he had a great, strong, and personal faith in God, and as you read his writings you discover this. On top of that, he knew how to laugh at his heartaches, but best of all, he knew how to read all his life. At age 12, he had read every book within a radius of 50 miles. He got into law because somebody couldn't pay a bill and they left him a barrel full of law books.

I called the publisher when I read a particular book about Lincoln that was no longer available. I said, "I want to buy 100 copies to give this to some of my friends." You know what they told me? It's out of print. Don't tell me it's out of print. I want 100 copies. He says, "It's out of print." I said, "All right, then reprint and I guarantee that people will buy every copy you print or I'll buy them all." So Tyndale House printed thousands of copies.

What Books Taught Me About Chambers' Life

I'd like to talk to you all day about books, but I would be remiss if I talked about excellence, and perspective, and my experience, and my management if I didn't mention Oswald Chambers. You say, "I've never heard of him." Well, it's no small wonder because Chambers died in 1917 at the age of 43. He never wrote a book. Well, how can you have 30 of his

Charlie "Tremendous" Jones

books if he never wrote a book? He married the Prime Minister of England's secretary, and when he went to work with the YMCA to work in Cairo, at the time of Gallipoli, she went with him and took her talent and made shorthand notes of everything he ever said. Now, when he died in 1917, she lived for years and wrote all the books from the notes she took. I tell my wife, "Honey, the world will never know how great a man I am. You haven't written down one lousy word I've said."

Let me tell you why I really love Chambers. Chambers had great insights about work. If he were alive today I'd love to hear him say, "Charlie, you can determine how lazy you are by how much inspiration and motivation you need to do something. If you're for real, you do it whether you like it or not." He says, "The best way to avoid work is to talk about it." Isn't that profound?

Reading Chambers has had a profound impact in my life. My wife will tell you had it not been for my love for

THE 3 THERAPIES *of* LIFE

Oswald Chambers insightful teachings, I could not love her the way I love her.

Regardless of who you are or where you come from in life, do not underestimate the power of books! Books. Never read just to be smart. Read to be real. Never read to be big. Read to be down to earth. Never read just to memorize. Read to realize. Never read just to learn more, but read to also unlearn. Some of the things you did learn weren't worth learning to begin with. Read just enough to keep yourself hungry and curious in getting younger as you get older if you really want excellence.

29 LIFE-CHANGING CLASSICS
Available at: www.tremendousleadership.com

7 Golden Rules of Milton Hershey (The), by Greg Rothman, collects the wisdom that set this great American industrialist apart from most of his robber-baron contemporaries.

Acres of Diamonds will help you to discover why Temple University founder Russell Conwell was referred to as the penniless millionaire and how he helped millions of others to tap into their potential through his famous Acres of Diamonds speech.

Advantages of Poverty, by Andrew Carnegie; Foreword by Dale Carnegie. Discover the attitude of selfless giving that motivated this innovative businessman to help various communities, charities and organizations achieve greater success.

A Message to Garcia, by Elbert Hubbard. A Message to Garcia, one of the keystones of American self-improvement literature, has carried its simple message of hard work, integrity and dependability to readers around the world for over 100 years.

As a Man Thinketh, by James Allen. Og Mandino counted *As a Man Thinketh* among the top ten success books of all time. All that we achieve and all that we fail to achieve is the direct result of our own thoughts.

Books Are Tremendous, edited by Charlie "Tremendous" Jones, documents the amazing impact that the reading of good books has had on great men and women throughout history. As you read the inspirational words by some of these influential individuals who have been transformed by the power of the written word, they will undoubtedly inspire you to develop a far greater appreciation for reading.

"Bradford, You're Fired!" is a timeless classic by William W. Woodbridge containing a provocative story of "The Super-self" that exists in every person who is willing to take an honest assessment of his or her life in order to make change for the better realizing every one of us is in business for ourselves.

Breakthrough Speaking, by Mark Sanborn. Anyone with the courage to speak publicly can deliver a speech, but breakthrough speakers inspire listeners to take action. If you have a message to deliver—one that you sincerely believe in—and your philosophy moves you to want to inspire and change people, the best way to reach them is by mastering *Breakthrough Speaking!*

Character Building, by Booker T. Washington. This practical book by the former slave and founder of Tuskegee Institute shares keys to character building taken from the notes he compiled related to his Sunday Evening Talks to students and teachers during the early days of the Institute.

From Belfast to Narnia: The Life and Faith of C.S. Lewis, by The C.S. Lewis Institute. In this brief introduction to his life and works you will uncover what inspired C.S. Lewis, what drove him and what experiences shaped the life of this extraordinary writer, theologian and friend of God.

Greatest Thing in the World (The). This classic book written by Henry Drummond, illuminates the importance of 1 Corinthians 13. Widely read and quoted for decades, it has sold millions of copies and continues to influence people to follow God's two great commandments: to love God and to love each other.

Key to Excellence (The), by Charlie "Tremendous" Jones. Filled with classic wisdom and humor, this easy-to-read book reflects Charlie's keys to excellence in leadership, ministry, home, and work.

Kingship of Self-Control (The), written by William George Jordan, is a book that will lead you expertly along the road of personal triumph by pointing the way to ultimate growth and happiness through self-discipline.

Lincoln Ideals (The), edited by Charlie "Tremendous" Jones. This remarkable, pocket-sized collection of excerpts and quotes in Lincoln's own words provides an inspiring insight into the mind of our greatest president.

Luther on Leadership, by Stephen J. Nichols. This volume in the Life-Changing Classics series outlines five leadership tenants of Martin Luther, the man whose theological trajectory allowed millions to find a personal relationship with God.

Maxims of Life & Business With Selected Prayers is a dynamic book that encapsulates the life and wisdom of John Wanamaker. The wisdom of the millionaire "Merchant Prince" who was the originator of the department store concept will undoubtedly inspire you to live your life to the fullest and for the benefit of others.

My Conversion. Charles Spurgeon's classic account of his coming to understand the plan of salvation, now available in our popular *Laws of Leadership* series!

Mystery of Self-Motivation (The), by Charlie "Tremendous" Jones. There are no barriers you can't overcome if you are learning to be motivated.

New Common Denominator of Success (The), by Albert E.N. Gray. The common denominator of success and the secret of success of every person who has ever been successful lies in the fact that he or she formed the habit of doing things that failures don't like to do.

Price of Leadership (The), by Charlie "Tremendous" Jones; foreword by Tracey Jones. Experience nonstop laughter as you experience this great humanitarian's ideas about life's most challenging situations in business and at home.

Reason Why (The), by R.A. Laidlaw; Introduction by Marjorie Blanchard. R.A. Laidlaw, a highly successful New Zealand businessman, shares his faith with his employees. *The Reason Why* is just as essential and compelling today as it was over ninety years ago.

Ronald Wilson Reagan: The Great Communicator, by Greg Rothman. A brief yet compelling biography by Greg Rothman that unveils the human being behind the man who magnificently played the role of leader of the free world.

Science of Getting Rich: Abridged Edition (The), by Wallace D. Wattles. Men get rich by doing things in a Certain Way; and in order to do so, men must become able to think in a certain way. A man's way of doing things is the direct result of the way he thinks about things.

Self-Improvement Through Public Speaking. Research has confirmed again and again that public speaking is essential to success. This practical guide by Orison Swett Marden will help you to understand the significance of gaining the verbal advantage needed for your career, personal and social life.

Succeeding With What You Have, by Charles Schwab; Foreword by Andrew Carnegie. Schwab had a deep appreciation for the common, dedicated working man and he gave the power to succeed to any employee who was willing to pay the price.

That Something, by William W. Woodbridge. That Something is real power as truly as the electric current...it is the power of the inner being, the fuel of the soul machine...it is the one thing necessary.

Three Decisions (The), Charlie Jones shows us that, when we clear away the clutter that fills our daily existence, we'll find that there are only three decisions that determine the course of each of our lives. What are they? Read The Three Decisions and find out!

Walt Disney: Dreams Really Do Come True!, by Jason Liller. Learn some of Walt's secrets of success in these pages, apply them to your life right now, and build a wondrous future for yourself, your company, and your family!

Wit and Wisdom of General George S. Patton (The), compiled by Charlie "T." Jones. The wit and wisdom of one of our greatest military leaders in a compact, highly readable edition!